Spiritual and Walking Guide

León to Santiago on El Camino

STACEY WITTIG

Wittig, Stacey
 Spiritual and Walking Guide: León to Santiago on El Camino
  1. Travel 2. El Camino
  ISBN-13: 978-0615989396 (Spiritual and Walking Guides)

DEDICATION

This book is dedicated to my Dad, who cheers me on to
follow the pathways of my heart; my Mom, who
encourages me to write about the adventure; and my
husband, Dan, who keeps my heart young.

CONTENTS

CONTENTS

ACKNOWLEDGEMENTS

To those pilgrims who have gone before and the compassionate *hospitaleros* that demonstrate just what it means to be the 'hands and feet of Jesus.

INTRODUCTION

Jesus calls you to join him on El Camino de Santiago. "Come," he said in John 1:39 as he walked along, "and you will see." Jesus seems to be saying, "Come along on this pilgrimage, and when you have completed the journey, you will see your world in a new light." We are all humble pilgrims on this path and many of us long for a closer walk with him. My prayer is that you will meet Jesus along your journey in a way that you have never met him before. Use this book to call out to him. Let the meditations help you be still and listen for what God has to say to you.

For in Jeremiah 33:3 he promises, "Call to me and I will answer you and tell you great and unsearchable things you do not know."

Several years ago when planning my first pilgrimage along El Camino de Santiago in northern Spain, I searched for a small personal devotional that I could easily carry with me as a daily guide for my spiritual journey. I was hoping for a book that would direct my path physically as well as spiritually. Since I would be walking and carrying all my belongings, I was interested in reducing the amount of "baggage" that would weigh me down. In my commitment to lightweight backpacking, I went so far as to cut off all the tiny labels from my clothes and gear. Consequently, I was looking for a sort of space-saving, lightweight three-in-one book: a daily meditation, a Bible and a way guide.

Three treks along the ancient pilgrimage route later, I offer this book to others that have been searching for such a mélange. The spiritual guide contains recommendations for daily starting and stopping points, distance information, meditations, appropriate scripture readings, questions for personal reflection, lodging suggestions and insider travel tips. While designed for pilgrims on El Camino, this lightweight manuscript is equally suitable as a spiritual guide for any trekking, biking or camping adventure. The scriptures cited here will guide any wanderer along the pathways of his or her heart.

Daily meditations include recommendations for where to sleep each night. These are mere suggestions. For me, a tentative plan for lodging is reassuring as I leave on a journey, but I always expect those plans to change. Perhaps the recommendations will give you reassurance, as well. However, I encourage you to move at your own pace by following the leading of your heart and spirit... or sometimes your physical body. Plenty of alternate opportunities will be revealed to you by other pilgrims, administrators at the *albergues* or by handouts found at visitor centers. Use my recommendations... or not. Remember that during busy times of the year (mid-May through mid-October), *albergues, refugios* and other accommodations fill up faster than at other times. Be open and flexible to change.

In this book you'll find space to document:

- the date,
- distance traveled and
- responses to questions for reflection

that makes this spiritual companion journal-like. Near the back of the book, pages are dedicated to recording fellow pilgrim's contact information. The size of this book was designed so you could keep it easily accessible in an outer pocket of your backpack or cargo pants.

As a lightweight backpacker, I have been known to tear out the section of the guidebook that I need, rebind it with duct tape, and leave what I don't need at home. From this experience, I have designed this series of guides in separately bound editions. You need only purchase and carry the small volume that covers the portion of the pilgrimage that you plan to traverse.

This volume encompasses the sections from the city of León, Spain, to Santiago de Compostela. If you are starting in León, Spain, or a town west of there, then this is the guidebook for you.

BEFORE YOU GO

God wants to spend more time with us, and we are blessed when he does. Then why is it so difficult for us to fit spiritual time into our demanding days? In our busy culture, we try to find places in our hectic schedules where we can slip in prayer, study and spiritual meditation.

Taking time to walk El Camino de Santiago, an ancient pilgrimage route, is one way to stave out the daily demands and spend time with God. By dedicating a week, ten days or several weeks, you can walk a portion of the route. If you like it, you can come back for more and walk a different section or *etape* as they are called in Spain and France. Pilgrimage routes begin all over Europe and terminate at Santiago de Compostela. The most well-known section to us in the 21st century is called *Camino Frances* that extends from St. Jean Pied de Port in western France to Santiago de Compostela in northeastern Spain. That route takes five to six weeks to walk, but not many businesspeople from the United States have that much vacation time accrued. That is why this series of meditations is designed for thirteen days of trekking. Daily meditations are included for days prior to your pilgrimage – so that you may prepare your heart. Readings are added for days following so you may debrief and continue the transformative experience once you are home.

Before you go, make arrangements for the head of your church or spiritual leader to pray the Pilgrim's Blessing over you (see page 90.) I recommend that you schedule a sending-out ceremony on DAY TWO of your readings, but you could do it at any time before you leave. Having friends and family around you for this blessing marks the start of your spiritual journey and could be a lesson in humility for you, too. (See DAY TWO reading.)

Prior to leaving home, make sure that you weigh your pack. We Americans pride ourselves in being prepared for anything but, unfortunately that means packing too much. I weigh my pack, take out items and reweigh many times before I leave. It's difficult for us to give up our "baggage," both emotionally and physically.

I limit my pack (without water) to 30 pounds/13.6 kilograms, but one expert recommends that you carry only 10% of your body weight. She challenges El Camino pilgrims to *walk further by carrying less* in her excellent book by the same name. Author Jean-Christie Ashmore suggests that each item which you have trouble leaving behind represents a fear. I've seen a whole roll of toilet paper packed for a three-day trek, eight sticks of lipstick stashed for seven days in the country and a laptop computer packed for a twenty-one day pilgrimage. What do those items say about the backpackers' fears? Let me know because I am the one who lugged the weighty Dell computer along El Camino for three weeks. When I checked into the Pilgrim's Office at St. Jean Pied de Port, the friendly hostess sighed, "*Ah, Stacey Wittig, la grande dame avec le grande sac.* The big woman with the big backpack." Two days later I was leaving behind gloves, brochures and a thick-as-a-brick electric converter. I hadn't realized when I left home that my Dell power cord had a built-in converter for European electrical service.

After the previous baggage dissertation, this next bit of preparation may seem counter-intuitive. Before departure, pick up a stone and put it in your backpack. The stone from your homeland symbolizes something that you want to leave behind on this upcoming journey. Perhaps you want to be healed or let loose an emotional or physical pain. Maybe you are burdened with unforgiveness or another sin. The stone symbolizes whatever burden that you hope to release sometime during your pilgrimage. You will have a chance to leave the stone at the foot of the iron cross, *Cruz de Fierro* near Foncebadón, Spain as other pilgrims have done over the centuries.

Make sure that you also bring along a headlamp, ear plugs and an eye mask for sleeping in pilgrim quarters. Believe me, you won't want to leave those essential survival items at the foot of the cross.

Insider Tip: When making your airline reservations, be sure to plan at least one full day in Santiago de Compostela after the day you arrive by foot and before the day you fly out via airplane.

HOW TO GET A PILGRIM CREDENTIAL

The Pilgrim Credential is the paper that you will carry with you along El Camino de Santiago to verify that you are, in fact, a pilgrim. The official document is your passport to *albergues* or *refugios* where pilgrims may stay overnight for the small donation or price of five to twenty Euros. Admittance to the *albergues* or *refugios* is granted by the credential which is then stamped by the hosts of the hostel-like abodes to prove that you made the trek. Stamps or *sellos* can also be obtained in churches, hostels, city halls and other places along the Way of St. James.

Order your Pilgrim Credential one to two months prior to your departure as it will be mailed to your home from one of these pilgrim confraternities:

American Pilgrims on the Camino
1514 Channing Avenue
Palo Alto CA 94303-2801
www.americanpilgrims.com/camino/credential_req.html

Australian Friends of the Camino
P.O. Box 601
Stirling, South Australia 5051, Australia
www.afotc.org

Canadian Company of Pilgrims
POB 57004
Ottawa, Ontario K1R 1A1, Canada
www.santiago.ca

The Confraternity of Saint James
27 Blackfriars Road
London SE1 8NY, United Kingdom
www.csj.org.uk/non-members-how-to-get-a-pilgrim-record-from-the-csj

If you do not have time to order ahead, Pilgrim Credentials may be purchased at approved locations along the way. For a list, checkout *http://bit.ly/1eebc5o*

Please note that *albergues* or *refugios* do not receive subsidies so pilgrims should help keep them neat and orderly. You are being received with Christian hospitality, and you should show respect to your hosts and fellow pilgrims. Brush up on "Pilgrim Etiquette" before you leave at *http://bit.ly/1eDECon*

HOW TO RECEIVE A COMPOSTELA

Once you arrive at Santiago de Compostela, take your Pilgrim Credential to the *Oficina del Peregrino*, the Pilgrim's Office, to receive your *Compostela*, the official certificate of the pilgrimage (see DAY SEVENTEEN.) The certificate written in Latin and inscribed with your name is only awarded to those who "have come in Christian terms: *devotionis affectu, voti vel pietatis causa* – motivated by devotion, vow or piety." Others receive a certificate of completion. A second prerequisite for the *Compostela* is that you walk the last 100 kilometres or cycle the last 200 kilometres of the pilgrimage route.

Since December 16, 2015, the Pilgrim's Office is at a new location:

> **Oficina del Peregrino**
> Rúa Carretas, no. 33
> 15705, Santiago de Compostela
> Tel: (+34) 981 568 846
> info@peregrinossantiago.es
> http://peregrinossantiago.es/eng

HOW TO FOLLOW THE ROUTE WITHOUT MAPS

The route along El Camino de Santiago is marked with yellow arrows and red and white flashes. You will also see a stylized scallop shell on a blue background. You won't need maps to follow the route if you look for the way markers on sidewalks, trees, sign posts and concrete pillars. They are usually posted at inconspicuous spots, but once your eyes get trained to see them, they are easy to follow. I always watch for them to make sure that I am on course. If somehow you lose your way, ask a local, *"Donde esta El Camino de Santiago?"* or simply *"El Camino de Santiago?"* with a quizzical shrug. They are used to lost pilgrims and will be happy to point you back on course (see DAY FOURTEEN.) If no one is near, go back to the last place where you saw a marker, say a prayer and start seeking the next yellow arrow or white shell all over again.

DAY ONE
Joy and peace, the balm for a stress-filled life

Day's Journey: Inner journey at home or in transit
Miles/kilometres: 0.0   **Date:** ___/ ___/ ___

Prayer to the Holy Spirit: Come Holy Spirit, fill the hearts of your faithful and kindle in us the fire of your love. Send forth your spirit, and we shall be created, and you shall renew the face of the earth. Oh God, who by the light of the Holy Spirit did instruct the hearts of the faithful, grant that by the same Holy Spirit we may be truly wise and ever enjoy your consolations through Christ our Lord. Amen.

Isaiah 55:11 You will go out in joy and be led forth in peace; the mountains and hills will burst into song before you, and all the trees of the field will clap their hands.
Isaiah 26:3 You [God] will keep in perfect peace those whose minds are steadfast, because they trust in you.
Pause for silent reflection.

Like many other Americans, my life was rushed and dictated by a calendar full of events. I felt trapped by my high-paying job. How could I possibly leave a career that provided prestige, success and every worldly comfort known to humankind? On the other hand, how could I survive inside the confines of busyness that created anxiety and crushed my spirit? Any peace that I could gather from my twenty-minute morning devotions was sucked away by the remainder of the next sixteen hectic hours.

I practiced stress-reducing habits learned at management seminars. Techniques like deep breathing at my desk, working out at the club every noon hour, keeping regular appointments with my psychologist, implementing every time-management tool that I could get my hands on, and meditating on God's word. Nevertheless, after years of multi-tasking and stress-reduction therapies, I felt more worn-out than ever. I was getting glimpses of peace during my morning devotion time, but I hungered for more. I had lost my joy.

Seven years ago, during a self-imposed weekend retreat, I heard the Lord whisper, "Walk El Camino de Santiago." El Camino hadn't crossed my mind for over a decade; and, in fact, I really didn't know much about the ancient pilgrimage route. Yet I felt the Lord's call to take a spiritual journey. The obedient act of walking would teach me to shift my emphasis from trust in a busy calendar to trust in God's provision. I had to let go of the belief that *if only* I had enough sales appointments, won enough sales contests, (fill in the blank with your own *if only*,) then I would be perfectly happy. I thought of myself as self-made, and relished the image of me – a working woman – pulling myself up by my own bootstraps, or in my case, by my own *Bandolino* Italian leather pumps.

I would start to loosen my fist clutched to my own efforts and begin to trust in the Lord. Sure, I trusted in the Lord that He was – that he existed. He could help me in the Big Things of Life, but although I prayed, "Give us this day our daily bread," my actions showed that I really didn't believe that he wanted to mess with small things like paying the bills… or providing daily bread. We all have grown up in a culture that honors self-reliance and self-control. It was – and is – very hard to make a paradigm shift away from control and towards a steadfast trust that relies on God to pay the mortgage, keep us safe and give us peace. For years, I had repeated the words, "Let go and let God." Now was the time to do it. I needed to step out in faith and explore the unknown path of St. James. I kept remembering God's promise to wipe away anxiety and give perfect peace to those who trust in Him.

In today's verses, God gives us the paramount stress-reducing habit: Trust in the Lord with a steadfast mind. However, change is not instantaneous, old habits are not broken easily. Transformation, for me anyway, has been a slow process.

Prayer: Lord, transform my heart. Give me peace. Help me to trust in you for the little things as well as the big things in life. As I walk along the ancient pilgrimage route, I will concentrate on giving you my stress and worry. Please take it away from me. I want to have a steadfast trust in you – help me to trust in you. Bless me with your perfect peace as I learn to trust you for all things. Amen.

For Reflection:

❑ What, if anything, makes you feel trapped by your life's circumstances?

❑ On a scale of 1-10, how good are you at letting go of your anxieties and letting God handle them?

❑ How would your circumstances look different if you could attain "perfect peace" by keeping your mind set on God and his pathway for your life?

Accommodations: home

Insider Tip: At the beginning of your devotional time each day, use the **Prayer of the Holy Spirit** to invite the Holy Spirit to join you. Jesus promised "…the Holy Spirit, whom the Father will send in my name, will teach you all things…" (John 14:26.) Jesus explained that the Holy Spirit as teacher and comforter would dwell inside us. And so invite him in so that he might help increase your understanding.

DAY TWO
Blessings for the road

Day's Journey: at home or in transit
Miles/kilometres: 0.0   **Date:** ___/___/___

Prayer to the Holy Spirit – page 91
Psalm 25:4 Show me your ways, O Lord, teach me your paths.
Psalm 25:9 He guides the humble in what is right and teaches them his way.
Pause for silent reflection.

"Lord, it's hard to be humble." Are you old enough to remember that old country western tune sung tongue-in-cheek by Mac Davis? If, not – no worries, I think you can relate; it *IS* hard to be humble. Humility is not part of our human nature. The opposite of pride, humility, must be learned. Often traveling affords conditions that can teach us humility.

I've been forced to be humble as a traveler on the Way of St. James. You must be able to bend to local customs and traditions. As a pilgrim, you can't always – as Burger King promises – "have it *YOUR* way." As a stranger in a strange land, you will be forced to ask for help. Many times you will hear yourself say, "Which way?"

My first lesson in pilgrim humility came when I asked my church family to gather around me to pray. You see, my pride makes it difficult for me to ask for help … I even find it difficult to ask for prayer support. Nevertheless, with mustered humility, I asked others to give me a sending-off, a public declaration of blessing for my journey.

15

In ancient times, pilgrims were sent out from their local churches with a blessing from their congregation. Priests of the Middle Ages recited the **Pilgrim's Blessing** and prayed over the pilgrim, his walking stick and backpack. The blessing, an ancient ritual, gave permission for a journey into the unknown and asked Christ to accompany the pilgrim into difficult situations.

Make arrangements for the head of your church or spiritual leader to pray the ancient blessing over you. You may find the Pilgrim's Blessing on page 90. Having friends and family around you for this blessing marks the start of your spiritual journey and could be a lesson in humility for you, too.

As the scripture says, God guides the humble and teaches them the way. If you want to be assured of God's direction, be humble enough to hear his directive. So take a step into humility now, and plan to have the legendary blessing for the road prayed over you. Follow in the footsteps of those who have gone before. Ask those gathered around to witness your first step as you set out towards the ancient path.

The Holy Spirit, our teacher and guide, can help us become humble and less prideful. Therefore, press into the Holy Spirit, ask for guidance and be open to being molded by God.

Prayer: Lord, you are the potter; I am the clay. I am open to your guidance. Show me your ways and teach me your paths as I travel with you along El Camino de Santiago. Help me slough off my pride. Bring people into my life along the way that will help in this transformative process. Help me to humbly follow the pathways of my heart. In the mighty name of Jesus' name I pray, Amen.

For Reflection:

❏ Am I humble enough to let God's voice be heard over the chatter inside my head?

❏ What practices could I incorporate into my daily life that will help me take time to listen for God's direction?

    ❏ Scripture reading ❏ Meditation ❏ Partaking in Holy Communion/Eucharist ❏ Listening to others ❏ Memorizing each daily scripture verse

❏ How could humility help God show me his way?

Accommodations: home

Insider Tip: Make copies of the Pilgrim's Blessing on page 90 and hand them out to the people invited to your send-off. Not only is it a thoughtful souvenir of your blessing, but it will help others remember to pray for you while you are on your pilgrimage.

DAY THREE
God's gift of courage when we fear the unknown path

Day's Journey: at home or in transit
Miles/kilometres: 0.0   **Date:** ___/ ___/ ___

Prayer to the Holy Spirit – page 91
Micah 6:8 What does the LORD require of you? To act justly and to love mercy and to walk humbly with your God.
Joshua 1:9 Be strong and courageous. Do not be terrified; do not be discouraged, for the LORD your God will be with you wherever you go.
Pause for silent reflection.

God is doing something. He has beckoned you to follow him on this life-changing pilgrimage to Santiago de Compostela. If you are like me, you may not understand why. Perhaps you're not even certain that it *is* God that is putting the desire in your heart. Personally, I had a lot of fear to overcome before I could embark on the unknown path. I prayed for the gift of courage, but ultimately leaned on human companionship to give me confidence. In the final weeks before departure, I asked my coworker Dannette to accompany me. My colleague couldn't walk for the full duration but would meet me later along my route in the village of Triacastela. We would walk into Santiago de Compostela together.

So what is there to fear? The verse from Micah makes it all seem pretty simple. Our instructions are to do what is right, be kind to others and walk along side of the Lord during this upcoming pilgrimage. Not much to fear there. However, I was soon to find out that following those simple instructions was not that easy. If we could incorporate those key behaviors during the pilgrimage, they would be transformational for our whole life journey.

Perhaps God put it in my heart to ask Dannette to accompany me, or maybe I was just so scared of going it alone that I couldn't fully trust that the Lord would be enough company. Was I unable to loosen my tight fist of control around my life, or did God prompt me to invite my friend? He knew my strengths and weaknesses. He also knew Dannette's needs at the time.

Either way, when I took my first fearful step out of my husband's car and onto the curb at Phoenix Sky Harbor International airport, my gift of courage was knowing that my friend would be following me to Spain in another week.

For Reflection:
❏ What are your fears concerning the unknown path? Pray for God to give you the gift of courage.
❏ What is God asking you to do or believe?
❏ What is your response to those requests?

_____

Accommodations: Sleeping on an airplane?

Insider Tip: On parts *of Les Chemins de Saint-Jacques de Compostelle*, a linking pilgrimage route that traverses southern France, *"Bon courage!"* was the sendoff called out by French women as I hefted my pack and left their villages. I loved their encouraging words that reminded me of Joshua 1:9. When I asked, they related that they felt like they could never attempt such a journey. *"Un pied à la fois,"* I said in broken French. One step at a time.

DAY FOUR
God's promise of protection

Day's Journey: in transit to León, Spain
Miles/kilometres: 0.0   **Date:** ___/___/___

Prayer to the Holy Spirit – page 91
Isaiah 43: 1-4 The LORD says… "Fear not, for I have redeemed you; I have summoned you by name; you are mine. When you pass through the waters, I will be with you; and when you pass through the rivers, they will not sweep over you."
Pause for silent reflection.

You may be feeling a bit of anxiety on the eve of your pilgrimage. Others have felt similar apprehension. But once they dug into the scriptures, they found comfort in the words of the Lord. God really does promise his protection to his people. Jesus is a compassionate friend and gentle guide. If you haven't taken Jesus to be your personal guide and savior for this journey, now would be a good time to do so. When you begin your pilgrimage as one of God's people, he promises to protect you along the way.

El Camino de Santiago, or the Way of St. James offers to the aware pilgrim hope, grace and fulfillment. In DAY TWO's reading, we studied a little about humility. You could put humility to practice today and tell God, "I want to be your disciple. I want to follow you. Jesus, forgive me. Jesus, save me. I am turning to you and trusting my whole life to you. Be the Savior and Lord of my life. Yes, Jesus, take over. Be everything. Save me. Forgive me. Transform me. Because you died for me, empower me to live for you. Please send your

Holy Spirit to help me learn more about you. In your name I pray. Amen."

Maybe you've already prayed that prayer, or maybe you're not ready to pray it. In any case, you could fling wide the portals of your heart.* The outward physical pilgrimage is symbolic of the inner journey of our Christian walk. We can choose either to roam in the darkness or to follow the path in the light of the sun. At times, we may find ourselves humbly asking for guidance, while at other occasions, we may need to open ourselves to others in ways we've never shared ourselves before. Ask God to make your heart a temple adorned with love and joy, for tomorrow we embark on our pathway to Santiago de Compostela.

For Reflection:
❏ What are some of your fears right now?
❏ God promises to protect you on this journey. How does that make you feel?
❏ What are some ways that you could 'fling wide the portals of your heart?'

*From Prussian hymn by Georg Weissel (1590-1635)

_____

Accommodations: Albergue Santa Maria de peregrinos de las Carbajalas, Benedictine convent, Plaza de Santa Maria del Camino, León, Spain. Tel: (+34) 987 252 866/ (+34) 680 649 289. (34) is the country code for Spain. Dial it only if you are outside of the country. The telephone numbers following in this book omit the country code.

Insider's Tip #1: During daylight hours venture inside the medieval Cathedral of León to view the glorious stained glass. At night, return to see the spectacular illumination of the outside of the gothic, creamy stone façade. In the morning, simply step outside the door and follow the yellow arrows that guide you along the pilgrimage route. (See page 10.)

Insider's Tip #2: Tomorrow just after the village of Virgen del Camino, you'll see a large information sign for pilgrims which describes your options. Take the scenic route via Villar de Mazarife which is slightly longer. The shorter path follows so closely to the highway that the roar of the traffic is deafening.

DAY FIVE
Listening for spiritual direction

Day's Journey: León - Hospital de Órbigo (via Mazarife)
Kilometres: 32km/32 cumulative
Miles: 19.9mi/19.9   **Date:** ___/___/___

Prayer to the Holy Spirit – page 91
Psalm 46:10 Be still, and know that I am God; I will be exalted among the nations, I will be exalted in the earth.
Pause for silent reflection.

Once your physical body gets into the rhythm of the walking pilgrimage, you hike without head knowledge that you are doing so. Walking becomes like breathing. Your mind is no longer cognizant of the fact that your feet are moving and your arms are swinging.

After a few days, your mind is "still" as your body moves. I enjoy this part of walking. I can pray or meditate on God's word. I can dream of the future, or spend time in the past reminiscing bygones. Or I can choose to stay in the present moment and keep my mind still and open to the Lord.

If I keep my head filled with dreaming, reminiscing or worrying, when will I be open and receptive to hearing the Lord? If I want to hear God, I need to spend time meditating on scripture, waiting and listening.

During the upcoming days, meditate – or center your mind – on the daily scripture. Practice keeping your mind still as you walk. I say "practice" because being still and listening are hard work. Listening sounds easy – we think of it as a passive activity. However, it is tricky to guard the mind and shut out wandering thoughts. One method to guard the mind is to concentrate on a word or phrase.

Some suggest that you find a word that has sacred meaning to you. For example, your word could be 'peace,' 'healing', or 'Jesus.' Meditate on the word by saying it aloud or to yourself over and over. My word is '*se ope me.*' The Latin word roughly translates as 'he helps me' or as I think of it: 'Hold me, support me, Lord.' I look for his comfort during my time with him. I want to lean on him for understanding. As I repeat my word, a distracting thought may come into my head. I acknowledge the thought, but let it slide by. It's as if I'm on an inner tube, floating along a slow-moving river. The disconcerting thoughts float by me, some faster, some slower than the speed at which I'm traveling. I let them bump off my inner tube. My thoughts are for another time and place. We *WILL* meet again. But now is the time to ignore these distractions and deny them entry into my mind. Now is the time I've set aside to be still and listen for God's voice.

For the first several days, you may be frustrated with this exercise. However, as you practice and train your spiritual ears, it becomes easier, just as it does while working-out physical muscles. Listen with expectation. Hearing the still, small voice of God does not come easily, but the fruits of hearing God's direction are tremendous. By taking time to listen, you are opening your heart and mind to what he has to say. Be still.

For Reflection:
❒ Which methods that help exercise your spiritual ears are you familiar with? Have you tried any? Does pride get in the way?

❏ How do you think practicing humility could help you in the passive process of listening?

❏ Think back to times when you heard God's still, small voice. Maybe jot them down below. What happened when you did or did not follow his direction? How did it make you feel?

_____

_____

_____

_____

_____

_____

_____

_____

_____

_____

_____

_____

_____

_____

_____

Accommodations: Albergue Verde, 76 Calle Fueros de Leon, Hospital de Órbigo, _oasis@albergueverde.es_
Tel: 689 927 926 _www.albergueverde.es_

Insider Tip: Walking before dawn makes the kilometres go by faster. It's cooler before the sun comes up and so you naturally go faster to keep warm. When I first began my journey, I took breakfast in the _albergue_ and got waylaid by interesting conversations with other pilgrims. That put a slow start on the distance to be gained and forced me to walk in the heat of the day. Later, I learned that getting up early and walking in the predawn gave me time to be alone and meditate. Good conversation always lay ahead when I stopped for _café con leche_. Leaving early gives you the option of a longer lunch if temperatures climb midday. However, be sure to respect sleeping pilgrims and abide by the "earliest arise time" set by individual _albergues_.

DAY SIX
Finding companions along the way

Day's Journey: Hospital de Órbigo to Astorga
Kilometres: 16.1km/48.1 cumulative
Miles: 10mi/29.9   **Date:** ___/___/___

Prayer to the Holy Spirit – page 91
Ecclesiastes 4:9-12 Two are better than one, because they have a good return for their work: If one falls down, his friend can help him up. But pity the man who falls and has no one to help him up! Also, if two lie down together, they will keep warm. But how can one keep warm alone? Though one may be overpowered, two can defend themselves. A cord of three strands is not quickly broken.

1 Corinthians 15:33-34 Do not be misled: "Bad company corrupts good character." Come back to your senses as you ought, and stop sinning; for there are some who are ignorant of God – I say this to your shame.
Pause for silent reflection.

When I left the United States solo, my parents and friends worried about me. "You are hiking through northern Spain *alone*?" they asked. My reply was an assured "I won't be alone – I will be with friends. I just haven't met them yet." However, when I first entered Plaza Regla in León, I still hadn't seen many pilgrims, and as I walked to *Hospital de Órbigo* the next day, I had not yet made many meaningful connections. You may be feeling lonely, or you may be enjoying the time alone. Or perhaps you have already met other pilgrims that have welcomed you into their circles. By this time into my pilgrimage, I was wondering, "Where are all my friends?"

Often we feel lonely because we've unknowingly created barriers that keep us separate from others. Typically, walls are built on the foundation of fear. We are the only ones that can reach around those walls to offer friendship and love. Only by reaching, can we receive love. Reaching is not a passive action – it involves motivation, physical activity and risk. Dare to engage with other pilgrims. I found that people asked, "Why are you walking?" Be ready to answer the question. Your answers may change as the passing days give you space for introspection. Continue to listen and share with others along the journey to start the process of love. Offer love before you receive it and soon others will be asking for your opinion, seeking you out for fellowship and sharing their love with you.

Soon this isn't the person whose annoying snoring kept you up for hours in the *albergue* last night. By asking for her name and inquiring as to the purpose of her journey, you have transformed her into a woman with a name who is walking through the grief process after the loss of her husband. Or maybe he is a father contemplating a more rewarding career.

You might ask yourself, "Why has the Lord put me together with this person in this time and this space?" What lesson will you learn from this encounter? Your perception of this person was transformed, but how will YOUR life be transformed by meeting this person?

Note that our second scripture warns us to choose our companions wisely. In the past, I've let myself get tripped up by hanging out with people that were better left behind. Pray for discernment as to whom you should walk beside and whom you should walk on by.

"Pity the man" or woman who is down and

needs help to arise. Reach out, one day you may be that person.

For Reflection:
❏ What fears do you hold that may be creating a barrier to intimacy with others?
❏ Why are you walking El Camino?
❏ Who is the person that has annoyed you on this trip? How can you reach out?

Accommodations: Albergue de Astorga, Plaza de San Francisco 3, Apto. 35, *asociacion@caminodesantiagoastorga* Tel: 987 616 034 *www.caminodesantiagoastorga.com*

Insider Tip: Have possessions in your backpack that are too heavy to carry, but you can't bear to discard? Then simply mail them to the post office in Santiago de Compostela. You'll need an ID to retrieve the package once you arrive. Address the parcel to:

> Your name
> Peregrino
> Lista de Correos
> 15780 Santiago de Compostela

DAY SEVEN
Don't trust in wealth

Day's Journey: Astorga - Rabanal del Camino
Kilometres: 20.4km/68.5 cumulative
Miles: 12.7mi/42.6   **Date:** ___/ ___/ ___

Prayer to the Holy Spirit – page 91
1 Timothy 6:17-19 Command those who are rich in this present world not to be arrogant nor to put their hope in wealth, which is so uncertain, but to put their hope in God, who richly provides us with everything for our enjoyment. Command them to do good, to be rich in good deeds, and to be generous and willing to share. In this way, they will lay up treasure for themselves as a firm foundation for the coming age, so that they may take hold of the life that is truly life.
Pause for silent reflection.

We learn early that not many pilgrims are trekking El Camino for religious purposes, but we do find that most are searching for clarification on one or more components of their lives. Pilgrims may be seeking answers about ending relationships, they may be healing from broken relationships or physical problems such as cancer, or they may be walking simply to experience a richer life. My first trek was an escape from corporate America. Yes, I felt the Lord had directed me to walk El Camino, but once here, I wrangled with the demanding business life that I left behind. "Should I return to its debilitating rigors once I complete this short stretch of pilgrimage? Will my body and spirit survive four more stress-filled years until retirement? Do I really have a choice?" I felt trapped by a high-paying six-figure job that was crushing my spirit. I walked in lockstep towards the dangling carrot of promised healthcare and monthly retirement checks.

My time on El Camino was a retreat from the incentives of corporate life and was a chance for inner reflection. Instead of rushing for the next appointment, I took time to observe the world outside of my overstuffed Franklin-Covey day-planner. Back home, my relationships were with like-minded, aggressive American businesspeople who gave me the same advice: press on to retirement regardless. Here on El Camino I made friends with people from all over the world who could guide me from different sets of expertise. French artists, British mothers and even a German clown might help me rediscover my calling. A kayak guide from Alaska and a trendy Korean nurse helped me see the world through younger eyes. Dutch grandfathers and Spanish priests shared God's wisdom. After walking for several days, I began to feel my anxiety sloughing away. I felt alive again. I discovered that walking in relationship with others and walking with Christ was the life that was truly worth living. However, could I really turn my heart away from my hope in wealth – the proverbial carrot – and put all my hope in God? I could try.

Prayer: Dear Lord, help us to put our hope in you. Fill us with the confidence that it is you, who richly provides us with everything. Transform our hearts by helping us to turn away from our own wealth-building agendas. You want us to be filled with joy, not anxiety. Please direct us in your paths because we want to "take hold of the life that is truly life." – your promise for each of us. In Jesus' name, Amen.

For Reflection:

❑ How has the Lord used other pilgrims to speak to you?

❑ Is there an issue that prevented you from fully experiencing "today?"

❑ Are you exercising your spiritual ears as discussed in DAY FIVE? If not, go back and reread about centering your mind on the daily scripture. What's grabbing your attention?

Accommodations: Refugio Guacelmo, Rabanal del Camino run by the Confraternity of St. James, no reservations, Tel: 987 691 901, *www.csj.org.uk*

Insider Tip: Wash your clothes and hang them in the back lawn of the *refugio* but get your laundry done in time for daily Vespers at the old village church. The monks that live in this village may be praying Gregorian chants at 7:00 p.m. Tomorrow you will climb the pass near Foncebadón and drop the stone, a symbol of your burden at the foot of the *Cruz de Fierro* (see page 6.) Rest well tonight.

DAY EIGHT
Feeding the fire

Day's Journey: Rabanal del Camino to Molinaseca
Kilometres: 24.9km/93.4 cumulative
Miles: 15.5mi/58.0   **Date:** ___/___/___

Prayer to the Holy Spirit – page 91
Isaiah 1:31 The mighty man will become tinder and his work a spark; both will burn together, with no one to quench the fire.
Pause for silent reflection.

Have you ever started a campfire? You begin by collecting small splinters of wood, dry twigs or other easily ignitable pieces from the forest floor. With these small pieces of tinder, you can get your fire going with a simple spark. Controlled campfires are good for cooking, warming a cold body or aiding in quiet meditation. (Can you remember a time when you gazed contemplatively into mesmerizing coals?)

Problems happen when the fire goes out of control. The small mound of tinder has the potential to ignite a forest, burn down a house or consume human life. Our addictions can do the same. I am addicted to work; for me, work can be all consuming. My obsession with being the very best at my job not only keeps me separated from God, but it also blocks intimacy with family and friends. Staying focused on customer needs and sales objectives did make me a "mighty man" in coworkers' and bosses' eyes, but my addiction left little time for relationships outside the business environment. After twenty-five years of feeding the fire of my career, most of my friends were from the office and were stoking fires of their own. As a result, when I burnt out under the spark of my all-consuming work, no one was there to squelch the fire.

My pilgrimage along El Camino was one way for me to break out of the obsession of my addiction and spend time reflecting on my life. Why was I working so hard? My peace and joy were gone. Were recognition awards, corporate bonuses and a six-figure income really worth the trade-off? Could I actually step out of the security that corporate America offered and trust God for my sustenance? What changes could be made to keep me in my career? Could I really let go of the control that I had over my own life and follow the path that God had in mind for me?

Prayer: Lord, help me to walk humbly along this path today. Help me to let go of the "mighty man" inside of me that looks for recognition in the world's eyes. Take away my obsessions – I give them all to you. I don't want anything to block intimacy with you or the people that I spend time with today. I invite you to walk with me this day. In the name of Jesus, I pray. Amen

For Reflection:
❏ What burns you out?
❏ How could you use this pilgrimage time to let go of obsessions or addictive behaviors?
❏ Where is the Lord directing you today?

Accommodations: Albergue Santa Marina, Avenida Fraga Iribarne, Molinaseca, Tel: 987 453 077, 615 302 390 *http://caminodesantiago.consumer.es/albergue-santa-marina*

Insider Tip: Overnight in smaller villages where *albergues* are easier to find than in large towns like Ponferrada. I feel safe walking alone into bars or restaurants in rural communities such as Molinaseca. However, if you need make a purchase, larger towns offer greater shopping options so run errands during the day as you pass through more populated towns.

DAY NINE
Searching for hidden treasure

Day's Journey: Molinaseca to Villafranca del Bierzo
Kilometres: 30.2km/123.6 cumulative
Miles: 18.8mi/76.8   **Date:** ___/___/___

Prayer to the Holy Spirit – page 91
Proverbs 2 My child, if you accept my words and store up my commands within you, turning your ear to wisdom and applying your heart to understanding, and if you call out for insight and cry aloud for understanding, and if you look for it as for silver and search for it as for hidden treasure, then you will understand the fear of the Lord and find the knowledge of God.

For the Lord gives wisdom, and from his mouth come knowledge and understanding. He holds victory in store for the upright, he is a shield to those whose walk is blameless, for he guards the course of the just and protects the way of his faithful ones. Then you will understand what is right and just and fair – every good path. For wisdom will enter your heart, and knowledge will be pleasant to your soul.
Pause for silent reflection.

During my turbulent twenties, I lived for a time as a spiritual refugee with a devout widow. In a bygone era, Mildred and her husband built the first airport at Grand Marais, Minnesota. A remote north woods town now, a frontier town then. Mildred and I studied Bible verses together every evening. We would read the verse slowly, pray for the Holy Spirit to reveal wisdom and ask for discernment as to its meaning for us at that moment.

"Where is the nugget of truth in this, Stacey?" she would ask. "You have to dig deep for that nugget of gold." Digging was a good analogy for both of us. You see, we were both rock hounds. We loved to drive up the North Shore of Lake Superior to stop at cold beaches and dig through beach pebbles in search of the red-ringed Lake Superior agate. Small, many no larger than the tip of our 'pinky' fingers, they were difficult to find on those vast beaches. Ah, but the pleasure and delight when we found a translucent, vermillion-colored nugget.

My Bible studies with Mildred were perhaps my first experience with contemplative prayer, though that is not what we called it. Not until twenty years later, when looking for a way to find balance and tranquility in the tumult of a stressful career did I learn about contemplative prayer. This method of prayer used by Benedictine monks since the fourth century is the slow, meditative reading of scriptures with the purpose of listening for the Lord's direction.

Proverbs 2 tells us that if we call aloud for understanding, and if we search for insight as for a buried agate or hidden treasure, then the Lord will give us discernment and guide us along a good path. The verse goes on to say that if that wisdom enters our hearts (the spiritual part of us), then the knowledge is welcome to our souls (the intellectual part.) The paradox is that we must have heart understanding before God's wisdom makes sense to our brains.

Prayer: Father, put a hunger in my heart for searching for hidden treasure in your scripture. Help me contemplate your words so I might hear from you today and every day. Please give me discernment and guide me. In Christ's name, Amen.

For Reflection:

❏ How do you find the nuggets of God's truth that are meant for you?

❏ When has the Holy Spirit quickened your heart, and a scripture has jumped off the page like never before?

❏ What does it mean to you when the scripture says: *"wisdom will enter your heart"*? How do you think that works?

Accommodations: Albergue de peregrinos Ave Fenix, Calle Santiago, 10, 24500 Villafranca del Bierzo. The reclaimed building materials that make up this flagship hippy-esque *refugio* will inspire your imagination.
Tel: 987 542 655, *www.alberg̲u̲e̲a̲v̲e̲f̲e̲n̲i̲x̲.̲c̲o̲m̲*
Insider Tip: Tomorrow's trek will be very strenuous. Arrange with the host at your *albergue* in Villafranca for your backpack to be transferred to O Cebreiro. Then carry only a daypack or grocery sack filled with your daily supply of food and water.

DAY TEN
Perfect peace through trust

Day's Journey: Villafranca del Bierzo to O Cebreiro
Kilometres: 28.4km/152 cumulative
Miles: 17.7mi/94.5   **Date:** ___/___/___

Prayer to the Holy Spirit – page 91
Isaiah 26:3 You will keep in perfect peace those whose minds are steadfast, because they trust in you.
Philippians 4:4-7 Rejoice in the Lord always. I will say it again: Rejoice! Let your gentleness be evident to all. The Lord is near. Do not be anxious about anything, but in every situation, by prayer and petition, with thanksgiving, present your requests to God. And the peace of God, which transcends all understanding, will guard your hearts and your minds in Christ Jesus.
Pause for silent reflection.

This is one of the most difficult stages of the ancient route. The path is steep and muddy as you climb to 4,242 feet/1297 metres, one of the highest spots along El Camino. The weather is often blustery on the mountain pass and in ancient times, the church rang its bell so pilgrims could find their way through the fog or snow. The charming village of O Cebreiro, built of gray granite and thatched roofs is only one of the great rewards of this tough hike.

Some pilgrims are afraid to let go of their belongings and let someone else be in control of their backpack for a day. Nevertheless, I recommend that you arrange for your pack to be transported up to O Cebreiro. It is fairly easy to do this; talk to the host at your *albergue* in Villafranca. Take a daypack or grocery

47

sack with food and water for this stretch, and meet your backpack at the top. Can you let go and let God? Trust in the Lord that your belongings will be there when you hoof it into O Cebreiro.

The climb to O Cebreiro could be symbolic of other life experiences for you. Sometimes life's difficult paths bring us to the long awaited "mountain top experience." In our search for peace, we can't always understand why we have to pass through difficulties. In fact, God says that his peace transcends understanding. Understanding does not bring peace, but trust in God will.

Prayer: Dear Lord, Help me trust you with all my heart. Fill my heart with trust. Help me give up the need to "understand" and figure out every little detail. In all my ways, I submit to you, even if I don't exactly understand what that means. I trust that when I submit to you, you will make my paths straight. (Proverbs 3:5-6) Thanks be to God.

For Reflection:
❏ What racket is going on in your mind that disturbs your potential for perfect peace?
❏ Visualize yourself releasing that hubbub to God. What stands in the way for you to trust him to take it?
❏ What are you thankful for today?

_____

Accommodations: Albergue de O Cebreiro, Pedrafita do Cebreiro, Tel: 660 396 809
http://camino.xacobeo.es/albergues/albergue-de-o-cebreiro
Insider Tip: Once you've conquered the climb to O Cebreiro make sure to explore the reconstructed ninth century pre-Romanesque church and seek out its Holy Grail. The miracle of the grail was so important that its image was integrated into the shield of Galicia. Watch for the shield in the days ahead as you walk through rainy Galicia along the way to Santiago.

DAY ELEVEN
Walking with Christ

Day's Journey: O Cebreiro to Triacastela
Kilometres: 20.9km/172.9 cumulative
Miles: 13mi/107.4   **Date:** ___/___/___

Prayer to the Holy Spirit – page 91
Luke 24:13-30 Now that same day two of them were going to a village called Emmaus, about seven miles from Jerusalem. They were talking with each other about everything that had happened. As they talked and discussed these things with each other, Jesus himself came up and walked along with them, but they were kept from recognizing him.

He asked them, "What are you discussing together as you walk along?" They stood still, their faces downcast. One of them, named Cleopas, asked him, "Are you only a visitor to Jerusalem and do not know the things that have happened there in these days?"

"What things?" he asked.

"About Jesus of Nazareth," they replied. "He was a prophet, powerful in word and deed before God and all the people. The chief priests and our rulers handed him over to be sentenced to death, and they crucified him; but we had hoped that he was the one who was going to redeem Israel. And what is more, it is the third day since all this took place. In addition, some of our women amazed us. They went to the tomb early this morning but didn't find his body. They came and told us that they had seen a vision of angels, who said he was alive. Then some of our companions went to the tomb and found it just as the women had said, but him they did not see."

He said to them, "How foolish you are, and how slow of heart to believe all that the prophets have spoken! Did not the Christ have to suffer these things and then enter his glory?" And beginning with Moses and all the Prophets, he explained to them what was said in all the Scriptures concerning himself.

As they approached the village to which they were going, Jesus acted as if he were going farther. But they urged him strongly, "Stay with us, for it is nearly evening; the day is almost over." So he went in to stay with them.

When he was at the table with them, he took bread, gave thanks, broke it and began to give it to them. Then their eyes were opened and they recognized him, and he disappeared from their sight. They asked each other, "Were not our hearts burning within us while he talked with us on the road and opened the Scriptures to us?"

Pause for silent reflection.

This is a story about the first Easter dinner. Two believers are walking cross-country, talking as they go. They are downcast; no Easter egg hunt this year. Jesus joins them, but they do not recognize him.

Read Jesus' words again and underline them if you can. Isn't Jesus a good listener? He asks probing questions to hear their version of the story – his story. There is a progression of his involvement in the discussion. He doesn't jump in and overrun the conversation. Yet he uses the walk as study time for Cleopas and friend. They enjoy his teaching so much that they invite him to stay for dinner. Only when he breaks the bread are their eyes open to who he is.

At the pilgrim's mass in Triacastela, I was asked to read this scripture in English. The story about this encounter with Jesus during a walk to the village of Emmaus is special to me since it is the basis for the Walk to Emmaus movement of which I am a part. The Protestant movement had its beginnings on El Camino when a Catholic lay leader brought pilgrims to study *cursillos*, or short courses in Christianity. Cursillos is now the name of an apostolic movement of the Roman Catholic Church.

During the pilgrim mass at Triacastela, other pilgrims read additional scriptures in their own languages, which is a sweet part of the Taizé services often conducted along El Camino. Taizé integrates people and cultures from across the world and incorporates meditative singing into worship. The memorable evening included rendezvousing with my Arizona friend, Dannette, and introducing her to my new Camino companions.

For Reflection:

❒ What walls might be up for Cleopas and his travel companion on this journey?

❒ What fears might you – like Cleopas – have that could hinder you from seeing and hearing God's voice while listening to a wandering stranger?

❒ How can you use Jesus' example of getting someone involved in a conversation? Perhaps your heart will be burning while you talk with others on the road today or tomorrow.

Accommodations: Triacastela, Aitzena albergue, 1 Plaza Vista Alegre _info@aitzenea.com_ Tel: 982 548 076 or 670 452 476 _www.aitzenea.com_

Insider Tip: King of Spain Philip II, for whom the Philippine Islands are named, slept here. On May 16, 1554 when Philip was a mere prince, he slept in Triacastela during his journey to England for his arranged marriage to Mary Tudor, the Queen of England. Millions of people have trod this route throughout the centuries. Famous pilgrims include St. Francis de Assisi, Queen Isabella, Pope John Paul II, Shirley MacLaine and Paulo Coelho. Let your footsteps mingle with theirs.

DAY TWELVE
Be prepared to give an answer

Day's Journey: Triacastela to Barbadelo
Kilometres: 28.9km/201.8 cumulative
Miles: 18mi/125.4   **Date:** ___/___/___

Prayer to the Holy Spirit – page 91
1 Peter 3:8-17 Finally, all of you, be like-minded, be sympathetic, love one another, be compassionate and humble. Do not repay evil with evil or insult with insult. On the contrary, repay evil with blessing, because to this you were called so that you may inherit a blessing. For, "Whoever would love life and see good days must keep their tongue from evil and their lips from deceitful speech. They must turn from evil and do good; they must seek peace and pursue it. For the eyes of the Lord are on the righteous and his ears are attentive to their prayer, but the face of the Lord is against those who do evil." *

Who is going to harm you if you are eager to do good? But even if you should suffer for what is right, you are blessed. "Do not fear their threats; do not be frightened." But in your hearts revere Christ as Lord.

Always be prepared to give an answer to everyone who asks you to give the reason for the hope that you have. But do this with gentleness and respect, keeping a clear conscience, so that those who speak maliciously against your good behavior in Christ may be ashamed of their slander. For it is better, if it is God's will, to suffer for doing good than for doing evil.
Pause for silent reflection.

*From Psalm 34:12-16

Peter was writing to persecuted Christians around A.D. 62-64. A sword had already killed St. James (Santiago) about twenty years earlier during the rule of Herod Agrippa. Christians were being tortured and killed for sharing their faith.

Today we don't fear death, but there is something about 21st century culture that makes us fear a fate worse than death when we consider sharing our faith. That happens even when we are on a Christian pilgrimage route. To waylay our fears, Peter gives us simple instructions: show sympathy, love your fellow pilgrims and be compassionate and humble. Can you hear Peter encouraging you, "Who is going to harm you if you are eager to do good?"

While you walk along, prepare your story so you can "give an answer" to anyone who might ask about your hope and faith. Maybe start the narrative by describing what you were like before Christ came into your life. Next, you could reveal how you came to be a Christ follower. Conclude your story by telling about the difference Christ is making in you now. Once you are comfortable with your narrative, shorten it up so you can tell it in a few sentences.

Now practice telling the story as you tramp along. You could be like St. Francis, who preached to the birds and animals. Rehearse your story by telling it aloud to the passing winged creatures. Pray that God would bring someone to you with whom you could share your story. Ask the Holy Spirit to show this person to you, and then tell your story with gentleness and respect.

Prayer: Thank you, Lord, that your ears are attentive to my prayers. Help me to prepare and tell my story of hope and faith. Amen.

For Reflection:
❏ What is intriguing about your story that would cause others to ask questions?
❏ What keeps you from sharing about your Christian walk?
❏ How can you overcome these hindrances?

Accommodations: Casa de Barbadelo, Vilei s/n –
Barbadelo *info@barbadelo.com* Tel: 659 160 498
www.barbadelo.com

Insider Tip: To ensure that pilgrims cover the last
100km on foot (and do not take the bus or taxi) the
Pilgrim Office asks that pilgrims get two stamps a day
for their pilgrimage within Galicia. If you began your
pilgrimage before Galicia, then one stamp a day will do.

DAY THIRTEEN
Investing in transformation

Day's Journey: Barbadelo to Portomarín
Kilometres: 18.1km/ 219.9 cumulative
Miles: 11.2mi/ 136.6   **Date:** ___/___/___

Prayer to the Holy Spirit – page 91
Matthew 25: 14-19 Again, it will be like a man going on a journey, who called his servants and entrusted his wealth to them. To one he gave five bags of gold, to another two bags, and to another one bag, each according to his ability. Then he went on his journey. The man who had received five bags of gold went at once and put his money to work and gained five bags more. So also, the one with two bags of gold gained two more. But the man who had received one bag went off, dug a hole in the ground and hid his master's money. After a long time the master of those servants returned and settled accounts with them.
Pause for silent reflection.

This El Camino adventure is your bag of gold. You are like an able servant trusted with your master's wealth of love, perseverance and self-control. To get up every morning, lace up your boots and embrace your backpack takes self-discipline. To walk tens or hundreds of kilometres, you must continue to press on towards the goal before you. However, you may have discovered over time that you need only muster enough gumption for a single step. You have learned by now that one step after one step brings about change in the inner self. Today it probably took less effort to take the morning's first step than it did on DAY ONE.

Just like developing the habit of walking, you can take this time of pilgrimage to cultivate other habits in your life. By means of small step by small step, you are growing in self-control. Like small but faithful deposits into a bank account, your steps are sacrifices that take you progressively forward to a transformed you.

You are investing countless progressive footsteps on this journey. What would you like the result of your investment to look like? How can you multiply your Master's riches today?

For Reflection:
❏ What habits would you like to pick up along the way?
❏ Which character flaws would you like to leave behind?
❏ What do you desire some of the outcomes of your pilgrimage to be?

_____

Accommodations: Pousada de Portomarín hotel, Av
Sarria, 27170 Portomarín, Tel: 982 545 200
www.pousadadeportomarin.es
Insider Tip: There are plenty of *albergues* in Portomarín,
but Dannette and I treated ourselves to the comforts of a
hotel room at Pousada de Portomarín. As special treats,
we soaked in deep European bathtubs and had our
laundry done by housekeeping.

DAY FOURTEEN
Walking in the good way

Day's Journey: Portomarín - Palas de Rei
Kilometres: 24.9km/244.8 cumulative
Miles: 15.4mi/152.1   **Date:** ___/ ___/ ___

Prayer to the Holy Spirit – page 91
Jeremiah 6:16-19 This is what the LORD says: "Stand at the crossroads and look; ask for the ancient paths, ask where the good way is, and walk in it, and you will find rest for your souls. But you said, 'We will not walk in it.' I appointed watchmen over you and said, 'Listen to the sound of the trumpet!' But you said, 'We will not listen.' Therefore hear, you nations; you who are witnesses, observe what will happen to them. Hear, you earth: I am bringing disaster on this people, the fruit of their schemes, because they have not listened to my words and have rejected my law…"
Pause for silent reflection.

This scripture reminds me of my first day walking El Camino. My eye was not yet accustomed to seeing the yellow arrows or other markings that pointed the way from sometimes-inconspicuous locations. I stood at a crossroads contemplating which way I should go. When I strode out to the left, a woman's voice called out from an apartment window three stories above, "*Va la manera equivocada. Vaya el derecho.* You are going the wrong way. Go right." I looked up towards the sound of the admonishment and saw nothing but an open window with its curtain catching the breeze. I stopped, trying to understand the words delivered in a language that was unfamiliar to me.

Sometimes life leads us to a crossroads, and we wonder which path is the good way. We might be trying to make a decision about a job, or which college to attend, or whether to marry, stay single or divorce. In any case, we don't often hear audible instructions like I did that day when I set out on the ancient path.

In the verse above, God says that we should ask for direction. If we ask and pray for discernment, often God will reveal to us the good way. His revelation comes through dreams, visions, words of knowledge, scripture and – as it happened to me – through others. We can check what we think is the answer from God by comparing it to scripture. God will never lead us in contradiction to what the Bible says. You could ask, "God, is this direction truly from you?" I don't make a significant decision without the divine directive being first confirmed by other scriptures that I may read throughout the week or month. I might ask trustworthy people what they discern about the guidance I believe may be from God. In addition, I look for a sense of inner peace. Ask yourself, "Do I have God's gift of peace about this?"

Whether your decision is big or small, God wants to be part of it. "Whether you turn to the right or to the left, your ears will hear a voice behind you, saying, 'This is the way; walk in it,'" reads Isaiah 30:21.

Prayer: All-knowing God, plant in my heart the desire to listen so that I can hear your voice more clearly. In the name of Jesus, Amen.

For Reflection:
❏ Underline the words "ask," "listen," and "hear."
❏ Describe a time when you heard God's voice.

❒ Consider what could improve your spiritual hearing.
❒ How do you determine if the prompting that you hear is really from God?

Accommodations: Albergue de Palas de Rei, Carretera de Compostela, 19 (Plaza Concello), Tel: 660 396 820, *http://camino.xacobeo.es/en/hostels/hostel-palas-de-rei*
Insider Tip: While in Galicia – the rainy section of El Camino – I wore a rain jacket from a reputable outdoor gear company, nonetheless, the intense rain prevailed, and I was soaked. Regrettably, my pilgrim credential inside a zippered pocket was sodden, and ink from stamps collected along the way ran together in a blue-black mess. Keep all valuables in Ziploc bags and buy a backpacker poncho if necessary.

DAY FIFTEEN
Keep my feet from stumbling

Day's Journey: Palas de Rei to Ribadiso da Baxio
Kilometres: 26.8km/271.6 cumulative
Miles: 17.9mi/170   **Date:** ___/___/___

Prayer to the Holy Spirit – page 91
Psalm 56:3-7, 12-13 When I am afraid, I put my trust in you. In God, whose word I praise – in God I trust and am not afraid. What can mere mortals do to me? All day long they twist my words; all their schemes are for my ruin. They conspire, they lurk, they watch my steps, hoping to take my life. Because of their wickedness do not let them escape; in your anger, God, bring the nations down.

I am under vows to you, my God; I will present my thank offerings to you. For you have delivered me from death and my feet from stumbling, that I may walk before God in the light of life.
Pause for silent reflection.

In the Middle Ages, pilgrims walked from all over Europe to Santiago de Compostela, starting their journeys from places now known as Germany, France or Italy. A few years ago, I walked along one of those ancient pilgrimage routes in southern France called *Le Chemin de St. Jacque*, The Road of St. James. At one small village, the local Catholic congregation supported a small *albergue* for pilgrims. Situated next to a private garden canopied with trees, it was a glorious hideaway. There, I reconnected with others I met earlier and introduced myself to two new middle-aged pilgrims. Beginning their walk in the previous town, this was the end of their first day. Magritte and Yvette were tired from carrying too much. (We pilgrims seem to start with heavy burdens and end up emptying our backpacks little by little as we journey onward.) After cleaning up and washing their clothes by hand in the sink, the women revived and became giddy with the newness of their big adventure.

Inside the parish "Youth Room" that doubled as our sleeping quarters, three of us pulled 3-inch, vinyl-covered mattresses from the closet and distributed them to others that were staking claims on the tiny floor. It was easy to see that these women were not on a religious pilgrimage. Yvette seemed uncomfortable around church icons and mocked the three-foot high brass Crucifix standing on a draped tablecloth – a makeshift altar in the teen ministry center. With bawdy laughter, Yvette hung her wet bra and panties over Christ's outstretched arms. She didn't seem to notice that even the nonbelievers widened their eyes in disbelief.

Outside, women from the church arrived and spread the outdoor garden table with a feast. An overflowing salad, bowls of buttered carrots from their gardens and crusty baguettes accompanied hot pork steaks and cheesy scalloped potatoes. A huge round of Brie and bowl of large apples picked from the neighborhood tree rounded the abundant provision. The parish priest stopped by and welcomed us with two bottles of local wine. The meal was given with warmth and not a penny was asked in return. Inside, the bra and panties still hung from Jesus' welcoming arms.

The next day I continued with pilgrims Pierre-Emmanuel and Robert along a picturesque, historic canal. Walking was difficult because the path ran in and out of boggy terrain. Sometimes a foot would break through the marshy peat and plunge ankle-deep into the water below. It was a trick to wrench your foot back out of the quagmire. "Take care," I warned my companions, "You could easily snap you ankle in this stuff."

Later, the blaring staccato of a nearby ambulance shrieked its warning. As night fell at the next *albergue*, we learned that Yvette had twisted and broken her leg in the bog. Now, I'm not saying that God allowed her to stumble – I don't know. But I am fairly certain that she was not praying to be under his protection. The journey is not easy – we need to be under the shelter of his wings.

Prayer: Lord deliver me from death and keep my feet from stumbling. In the name of your son, Jesus, who welcomes each one of us to his table, no matter what our past.

For Reflection:
❏ How does this story symbolize your spiritual quest? Are you like the parishioners, serving without expecting payback? Are you more like the pilgrims distributing mattresses and helping others find comfort? What part of you is similar to the new pilgrims, oblivious to the sacred that surrounds you?
❏ How has God kept your feet from stumbling?
❏ What thank offerings can you present to the Lord today?

Accommodations: Ribadiso da Baxio albergue next to the river and medieval bridge Tel: 981 501 185 *http://caminodesantiago.consumer.es/albergue-de-ribadiso-da-baixo*

Insider Tip: Arzúa is known for its soft and creamy Arzúa-Ulloa cheese. Buy some for tomorrow's lunch and savor the produce from local farms.

DAY SIXTEEN
Heart connection

Day's Journey: Arzúa to Arca-O Pedrouzo
Kilometres: 18.4/292 cumulative
Miles: 12.4mi/181.4   **Date:** ___/___/___

Prayer to the Holy Spirit – page 91
Psalm 51:10-12 Create in me a pure heart, O God, and renew a steadfast spirit within me. Do not cast me from your presence or take your Holy Spirit from me. Restore to me the joy of your salvation and grant me a willing spirit, to sustain me.
Psalm 139:23-24 Search me, O God, and know my heart. Test me and know my anxious thoughts. See if there is any offensive way in me and lead me in the way everlasting.
Pause for silent reflection.

Sometimes I hear God's still small voice during meditation or worship and other times I clearly see the Holy Spirit's direction while reading scriptures. However, every so often I feel as if I have lost my connection to God. Maybe the path before me is unclear even after fervent prayers that seek his guidance. Eventually it dawns on me, "Maybe I have unrepented sin. What is it, Lord? Bring to mind that which I need to confess." I find that unrepented sin blocks my fellowship with the Almighty. When I finally realize that I am blocked, I look to my heart for exactly what it is I need to confess. I covet my heart connection with the Lord and so I ask him to reveal those things that are hindering the relationship.

The blockage is not always revealed to me and so then I pray, "Forgive me my sins both known and unknown." I am continually amazed by how the Lord is faithful and just to forgive my sins and cleanse me from unrighteousness (1 John 1:9.) Soon I am hearing his voice and enjoying a reunion on his everlasting pathway. If you feel like you need to renew your heart connection with God, try praying a confession. You could pray as you walk along, lift your repentance in a dimly lit church or spend some time alone in contemplation elsewhere.

Prayer: Most merciful God, we confess that we have sinned against thee in thought, word and deed, by what we have done, and by what we have left undone. We have not loved thee with our whole heart; we have not loved our neighbors as ourselves. We are truly sorry, and we earnestly repent.

For the sake of thy Son Jesus Christ, have mercy on us and forgive us; that we may delight in thy will, and walk in thy ways, to the glory of thy Name. Amen.
–From Book of Common Prayer

For Reflection:
❏ When you look inside yourself, what do you see?
❏ Search your heart, is there something that you want to confess to God?
❏ Thank God for cleansing you of all sin. Ask God to give you spiritual discernment to recognize sin that is generally accepted by our culture, such as "white" lies, "fooling around," or "over indulging."

Accommodations: Arca-O Pedrouzo, Albergue Edreira, Rúa da Fonte, 19 – Arca, O Pino *info@albergue-edreira.com* Tel: 981 511 365 *www.albergue-edreira.com*

Insider Tip: In the ancient of days, pilgrims ditched their worn out clothes and washed up at Lavacolla just a few kilometres down the road. They were readying for their entrance into Santiago de Compostela and the grand pilgrim cathedral. Perhaps this would be a good spot to splurge on using a washing machine to do the same.

DAY SEVENTEEN
Ecstatic joy

Day's Journey: O Pedrouzo to Santiago de Compostela
Kilometres: 20.1km/312.1 cumulative
Miles: 12.5mi/193.9 **Date:** ___/___/___

Prayer to the Holy Spirit – page 91
Psalm 100 Shout for joy to the Lord, all the earth.
Worship the Lord with gladness; come before him with
joyful songs. Know that the Lord is God. It is he who
made us, and we are his; we are his people, the sheep of
his pasture. Enter his gates with thanksgiving and his
courts with praise; give thanks to him and praise his
name. For the Lord is good and his love endures forever;
his faithfulness continues through all generations.
Pause for silent reflection.

This day was a difficult one for me. I wanted to arrive; I
pictured myself walking through the city gates of
Santiago de Compostela with joy filling my heart,
perhaps angels would break out in song. My
anticipation had been building after so many days of
walking, and I was keen to accomplish the goal that was
set before me. However, my walking companions were
not as eager as me. They stopped for what seemed like
an excruciatingly long coffee break in the morning.
While I wanted to eat lunch inside the gates of
Compostela, they petered out and ate a time-consuming
midday feast in the suburbs.

After all these days of pilgrimage, I still had not
peeled off my Type A personality. I wanted to run the
race, but I also wanted to stick with my friends that had
become so endeared and share the joy of entering the

gates with them. I poked along at the slowing pace of those apprehensive about the journey's end. When we finally did walk into *Praza do Obradoiro*, pilgrims who I met earlier along the way stood cheering. Many I had not seen for weeks, but there they were, familiar faces of fellow seekers rooting for me. My eyes filled with tears, a symptom of ecstatic joy filling my heart. I entered through the gates of the cathedral with thanksgiving in my heart and entered into his courts with praise.

For Reflection:
❐ What was today's greatest moment of joy? What experience was not so joyful?
❐ What has God been doing in your life since you began this journey?
❐ What lessons have been emerging along the way and how will you help them transform you?

Accommodations: Like any tourist destination city with a population of over 95,600 souls, Santiago de Compostela offers a wide variety of lodgings from the five-star *Parador de Santiago* to family-run guest houses to humble hostels. Pick your abode at
www.santiagoturismo.com

Insider Tip: Where to get your *Compostela*? Take your stamped credential to the Pilgrim's Office, which is a short distance from the Cathedral to obtain your *Compostela*. Follow the signs to Rúa Carretas, 33. The *Compostela*, the official certificate of the pilgrimage written in Latin, is only bestowed on pilgrims motivated by spiritual "devotion, vow or piety." Others receive a certificate of completion.

DAY EIGHTEEN
Prayer of protection

Day's Journey: around town
Kilometres: 0.0km/312.1 cumulative   **Date:** __/__/__
Miles: 0.0mi/193.9

Prayer to the Holy Spirit – page 91
Psalm 5:11-12 But let all who take refuge in you be glad; let them ever sing for joy. Spread your protection over them, that those who love your name may rejoice in you. Surely, Lord, you bless the righteous; you surround them with your favor as with a shield.
Pause for silent reflection.

I try to picture what it looks like to be surrounded with so much of God's favor that it becomes a shield. The Lord's favor would be woven around me, thickly covering me in a fluffy blanket of protection. I imagine that the shield is comfortable on my side, but is tough and durable on the outside to protect me from Satan's fiery darts. While walking this pilgrimage, you have most probably found refuge in God. The scripture above says that if you have, then you should be glad and sing for joy. Wrap yourself in that joy, rejoice in his comfort and feel his presence as you explore Santiago today.

I can bet that you have experienced deliverance from perilous situations, divine guidance and some sort of transformation that has deepened your trust in God. Let your heart be revived by his words above, take on the shield of favor and carry it home with you. Continue your walk with God as you return to the "real world," taking up your new habits and leaving behind the behaviors you detest. This scripture is a great benediction for sending you on your way back home under a blanket of protection.

Prayer: Our gracious Guide, thank you for spreading your protection over me. Please continue to do so as I make my way back home. I pray as Jesus taught us, saying "Our Father in heaven, hallowed be your name, your kingdom come, your will be done, on earth as it is in heaven. Give us today our daily bread. And forgive us our debts, as we also have forgiven our debtors. And lead us not into temptation, but deliver us from evil, for yours is the kingdom and the power and the glory forever. Amen." (Matthew 6:9-13)

For Reflection:
❒ What does a "shield of favor" look like to you?
❒ Describe some incidents on El Camino when you acted justly, loved mercy or walked humbly with your God.
❒ On a scale of 1-10, how good are you at letting go of your anxieties and letting God handle them?
❒ How does this rating compare to how you rated yourself on DAY ONE?

Accommodations: Choose yours at
www.santiagoturismo.com.
Insider Tip: Arrive early at the Cathedral for the
Pilgrims' Mass because the mass – usually held at noon –
can get crowded. You won't want to miss the reading of
the list of pilgrims who were received in the Pilgrim's
Office within the prior twenty-four hours. You won't
hear your name, but you will recognize yourself when
they read the number of pilgrims that arrived by
country. I was fortunate to experience the *botafumeiro*, a
five-foot-tall incense burner that zipped right over our
heads. To send it flying, eight men grappled with the
ropes tied to the behemoth incense burner.

DAY NINETEEN
Homeward bound

Day's Journey: in transit
Kilometres: 0.0km/312.1 cumulative   **Date:** __/__/__
Miles: 0.0mi/193.9

Prayer to the Holy Spirit – page 91
Luke 2:29-32 Sovereign Lord, as you promised, now dismiss your servant in peace. For my eyes have seen your salvation, which you have prepared in the sight of all nations: a light for revelation to the Gentiles, and the glory of your people Israel.
Luke 23:46 Into thy hands, O Lord, I commend my spirit
Pause for silent reflection.

Simeon, an old man, waited in the temple for the coming of the Messiah. The Holy Spirit had revealed to him that he would not die before he had seen the Lord's redeemer. I don't know how many times he was moved by the Holy Spirit to walk to the temple, but each time he walked expectantly and obediently. His patience and trust proved good when one day after walking the familiar way, he saw Mary and Joseph in the temple sacrificing two small birds for the rite of purification of the mother. As told in Luke 2:21-35, the Holy Spirit revealed to Simeon that the child with them was the Messiah, the one for whom he had been waiting. The old man took the almost-six-week-old Jesus in his arms and – using the words quoted in the scripture above – proclaimed that this indeed was the Christ child, the Light of the World. Simeon could now go on his way and die in peace.

Today, Benedictine monastics sing Simeon's affirmation as a prayer at the end of the day. His words also make a meaningful ending to a completed pilgrimage. The verse assures us that the light of the world is promised to all nations, from which many of your fellow pilgrims come. Take the promises that God has whispered to you along the journey and go in peace.

Find comfort in knowing that this ending creates a new beginning. Now, as you journey homeward, you start down the pathway of the next stage of your life. For this reason, begin this next journey rejoicing, "[I] will go out in joy and be led forth in peace; the mountains and hills will burst into song before [me], and all the trees of the field will clap their hands," (Isaiah 55:12) just as you began DAY ONE of this El Camino pilgrimage.

For Reflection:
❏ Following Simeon's example, can you be expectant about something as you walk out the next stage of your life? How could walking "expectantly" help you walk obediently?
❏ In what ways has this journey transformed you?
❏ What practices can you put into place to help make the transformation "stick?"

Accommodations: in the seat of an airplane
Insider Tip: Write down as many memories as you can during your trip home. I've found that the seat of an airplane is one of the best places to capture those scurrying thoughts. You don't need to write in complete sentences. Avoid correcting your grammar or spelling; that will stop the flow. Just push out the words as fast as you can and capture them on paper or in your electronic device. Your recollections will never be so close to your heart as they are right now. Buen Camino!

MORE RESOURCES

Ashmore, Jean-Christie, **Camino de Santiago: To Walk Far, Carry Less,** *http://amzn.to/1T7r2QJ*

Camino Planner, an online interactive planning tool that helps you set your own itinerary. You select the start and finish places and then it gives between-towns distances in miles or kilometres, accommodations and number of beds per *albergue* with sunrise/sunset times for the dates you pick. Download your plan to Excel, GIF, GPX, HTML, KML, PDF or PNG.
http://www.godesalco.com/plan/frances

Cathedral of Santiago de Compostela, official website
http://www.catedraldesantiago.es

Cursillos in Christianity, a Roman Catholic movement that enables Christians to discover their own unique, original and creative giftings. Born on El Camino de Santiago in 1944, the movement has spread to other Christian denominations across the world.
http://www.cursillo.org

Frey, Nancy Louise, **Pilgrim Stories: On and Off the Road to Santiago, Journeys Along an Ancient Way in Modern Spain,** *http://amzn.to/1eklVx5*

Gitlitz, David M. and Davidson, Linda Kay, **The Pilgrimage Road to Santiago: The Complete Cultural Handbook,** *http://amzn.to/1R5IsQ8*

Just Get Me Started, personalized guide service
www.thecaminoexperience.com

Keating, Thomas, **Open Heart Open Mind: The Contemplative Dimension of the Gospel,** Continuum Publishing Co, New York, NY, 1992.

Merton, Thomas, **Contemplative Prayer,** Image Book by Doubleday, New York, NY, 1996.

Pilgrims' Office, Santiago de Compostela, official website
http://peregrinossantiago.es/eng

Pilgrim Associations, see pages 7-8.

Taizé, an ecumenical monastic order and movement that seeks to include people and traditions from all over the world in prayer, worship and song.
www.taize.fr/en

Walk to Emmaus, a Christian renewal and formation movement that empowers leaders to be the hands and feet of Christ. Spun out of the Cursillos Movement for those of Protestant faiths, it supports people who wish to continue their faith journey.
http://emmaus.upperroom.org

THE APOSTLES' CREED

I believe in God, the Father almighty,
    creator of heaven and earth;

I believe in Jesus Christ, his only Son, our Lord.
    He was conceived by the power of the Holy Spirit
        and born of the Virgin Mary.
    He suffered under Pontius Pilate,
        was crucified, died, and was buried.
    He descended to the dead.
    On the third day he rose again.
    He ascended into heaven,
        and is seated at the right hand of the Father.
    He will come again to judge the living and the dead.

I believe in the Holy Spirit,
    the holy catholic Church,
    the communion of saints,
    the forgiveness of sins
    the resurrection of the body,
    and the life everlasting. Amen.

Book of Common Prayer, public domain

PILGRIM'S BLESSING

Lord, you who called your servant Abraham out of the
town of Ur in Chaldea
And who watched over him during all his wanderings;
You who guided the Jewish people through the desert;
We pray for you to watch your servants, who for the
love of your name make a pilgrimage to Santiago de
Compostela.

Be for us:
a companion on our journey
the guide on our intersections
the strengthening during fatigue
the fortress in danger
the resource on our itinerary
the shadow in our heat
the light in our darkness
the consolation during dejection
and the power of our intention

so that we under your guidance, safely and unhurt, may
reach the end of our journey,
and strengthened with gratitude and power, secure and
filled with happiness,
may join our home, for Jesus Christ, Our Lord, Amen.

Pilgrim's Prayer, The Priest's Prayer Book, 1864

PRAYER TO THE HOLY SPIRIT

Come Holy Spirit, fill the hearts of your faithful and kindle in us the fire of your love. Send forth your spirit, and we shall be created, and you shall renew the face of the earth. Oh God, who by the light of the Holy Spirit did instruct the hearts of the faithful, grant that by the same Holy Spirit we may be truly wise and ever enjoy your consolations through Christ our Lord. Amen.

Mass of the Holy Spirit, public domain

QUICK REFERENCE

FELLOW PILGRIMS' CONTACT INFO

Name	Email	Phone	Address

FELLOW PILGRIMS' CONTACT INFO

Name	Email	Phone	Address

ABOUT THE AUTHOR

Award-winning travel writer Stacey Wittig has walked over 1600 kilometres on Camino pilgrimage routes in Spain and France. Years of backpacking experience coupled with her love of the Lord makes a winning combination for those looking for a lightweight, all-in-one, daily devotional and walking guide for El Camino de Santiago pilgrimages. Wittig, who has written about her trekking adventures in India, New Zealand, Tanzania, Peru, Canada and the United States, uses the Apostles' Creed found on page 89 as the roadmap for her walk with Christ. The spirit-led believer writes from her Arizona home near the Grand Canyon.

Spiritual Walking Guides
P.O. Box 17032, Munds Park, AZ 86017
www.SpiritualWalkingGuides.com

HOW TO ORDER

Spiritual Walking Guide: León to Santiago is available in paperback from Amazon.com and other retail outlets, and is available for Kindle and other devices.

www.amazon.com/author/staceywittig